SNAKE E-OIL
THE SEO SWINDLE

How to Deal with SEO "Experts":
What to Do. What to Expect.

Luis Hernandez, Jr.
www.LuisHernandezJr.com

DISCLAIMER

The information presented in this publication is for entertainment purposes only. This book is the result of the author's experience and opinion. The author and publisher, therefore, specifically disclaim any liability resulting from the application of any of the ideas presented in this work. The information is not intended to serve as professional advice relating to specific situations.

Edited by Karen Aldridge
www.elance.com/s/edit/karen_aldridge/

Cover Design by Lacey O'Connor
www.laceyoconnor.com

ISBN-13: 978-1495288081

ISBN-10: 1495288080

Contents

Contents

"We dance round in a ring and suppose,
but the secret sits in the middle and knows."

—Robert Frost

For Pam

*"They'd been two souls searching for each other,
one spirit looking for the other."*

INTRODUCTION

The topic of SEO, or search engine optimization, is a difficult one to tackle, especially for newcomers to e-commerce and the web in general.

Anyone can make the claim of being an SEO expert as qualification requirements are up to the claimant, and the field itself is in constant flux.

Having been involved with the online world since the early days, I've lived through a changing web landscape as far as search engines are concerned. I have also dealt with my share of con men posing as SEO experts.

During my fifteen-year involvement with e-commerce as the owner and Webmaster of a small business, I realized web surfers would find their way to my store eventually, and if they were the right demographic, I would be able to sell them product.

From 1997, when I launched my web store, until 2013, when I sold the business, my small enterprise serviced more than six hundred thousand customers.

During that decade and a half, I owned a profitable business, and I learned a few things about what motivates people to buy online.

Store traffic is crucial, of course, whether you have a bricks-and-mortar or an online store. If you don't have customers to sell to, nothing will happen.

And this is part of the problem I have with SEO "experts." They make it sound like by just having visitors, all your problems will be solved.

Visitors are nice, but in order to be successful you need *customers*!

The truth of the matter is that if you attract the wrong kind of traffic, you may end up facing bigger problems: search engines may question the value of your site, which can result in your organic listing being buried down the list.

Most of us are well aware of the fact that very few people look beyond the first two pages on any given search engine. So if your listing is past page two, you won't derive benefit from it.

I will, however, tell you how you can make sure your listing appears on the first page on Google for the right search term, and it is something you can do yourself very quickly and without the assistance of an SEO expert.

I will also share lessons I learned while dealing with people who do search engine optimization, so you can avoid some of the potholes you'll run into if you decide to travel down that road.

So get ready for an interesting ride.

Luis Hernandez, Jr.
Orange City, Florida

WHAT IS SEO?

Let's see what the definition of SEO is, according to Wikipedia:

> **Search engine optimization (SEO)** *is the process of affecting the visibility of a website or a web page in a search engine's "natural" or un-paid ("organic") search results. In general, the earlier (or higher ranked on the search results page), and more frequently a site appears in the search results list, the more visitors it will receive from the search engine's users. SEO may target different kinds of search, including image search, local search, video search, academic search, news search and industry-specific vertical search engines.*
>
> —"Search engine optimization," *Wikipedia,* http://en.wikipedia.org/wiki/Search_engine_optimization

In essence, SEO means making changes to a website, both on and off the page, in order to generate more web traffic.

But when optimization is taken to the extreme or done incorrectly, Google penalizes offending sites by either banning them completely from their index or, alternatively, burying them far down the search engine results pages which, essentially, serves the same purpose.

But to be fair, you can't really fault humans for acting, well, like humans. We are conditioned to excel, we like to win, we want to make more money, and so on.

So SEO and search engines were destined to collide the moment someone realized that by stuffing lots of keywords on a web page, that page would shoot up the rankings.

However, search engines— especially Google—constantly improve their algorithms in order to try to exert some control over overoptimized websites. This means that techniques that worked last year will not work today.

As algorithms have gotten smarter, the amount of effort required to game the system is no longer practical. This is good news as it means that you will not need the services of self-proclaimed SEO "experts" who constantly troll the web in search of business.

I know that there are many capable and knowledgeable individuals who understand search engines and their associated algorithms better than 99.9 percent of the world population. No question about it.

Some of those capable individuals offer SEO services. But it is also my contention that, for the most part, they are busy working for large clients with deep pockets.

I also believe that these few take more of a global approach to their clients' web properties rather than focusing on the basic stuff like on- and off-page optimization. I say "basic" because most of us can do that, with varying degrees of success, of course.

The remaining "experts" are the ones I refer to as snake e-oil peddlers. Stay away from them!

SEO "GURUS"

If anyone you plan to deal with claims to be a "guru"—of any kind—run in the opposite direction! True experts in their field don't need to resort to trickery. Frankly, when I hear the word "guru" associated with SEO, I instantly think *charlatan*.

Yet SEO "gurus" like to brag about themselves, which is a good thing as it allows you to identify and avoid them.

On the other hand, if someone I trust has positive results after using a professional who truly knows and understands search engines, I would be open to getting more information.

CAN YOU OPTIMIZE YOUR OWN SITE?

Of course you can.

You need to have a basic understanding of best practices as specified by the main search engines, but mostly you will need to use common sense.

Most Webmasters, at some point, started chasing Google SERPs (search engine results pages) instead of focusing on making their sites stand above the competition.

They forgot to study their site analytics in order to determine which pages were ranking well and which were ranking poorly. Suddenly, all of their pages had to be at the top of the SERPs.

No one can make that claim today. Not Amazon, Wikipedia, eBay, Walmart, or any other company. So why do you think yours should be number one for every item you sell?

I mentioned in the introduction that I would tell you how to get your listings on the first page of Google for the right search terms, and I don't want to keep you waiting.

You might be familiar with AdWords—simply buy an ad and your website will appear on that first page when someone searches for your targeted keywords. That's it!

GOOGLE'S FIRST PAGE

Once upon a time…

Google's first page sounds like a fairy tale today. Why? Because two people searching for the same item, using the same keywords will—most likely—get different organic results.

If you happen to have a Google+ account, search for anything on Google and note or take a screen shot of what you see. Then log off, conduct the exact same search and compare the results. Chances are they will be different. Sometimes slightly, other times noticeably.

Google's algorithms are serving search results based on who you are, where you are located, past searches, which sites you have visited in the past, and more.

Why do you think they want people to use Google Chrome? That's their browser, and every time we use it, we are telling Google a little bit more about ourselves, our habits, our likes and dislikes, our hobbies, sites we visit often, and so on.

And we tell Google even more about ourselves the moment we log on to Gmail or Google+. It's kind of scary, isn't it?

Of course this can also be seen as a positive thing, as long as Google uses its "super powers" for good, not evil.

So the next time an SEO "expert" tells you his or her company can make your site come up on Google's first page, now you know.

ON-PAGE SEO

On-page SEO was really effective from 1995 to around 2005. After 2005 its effectiveness has been greatly reduced, and in cases where it gets abused, it's a bad signal to search engines.

I am not saying you can just type whatever you want on a web page and expect good results, even when using AdWords. Search engines have become smarter over the years, and on-page SEO is not what it used to be.

Write content for your customers, and stop worrying about keyword density and other nonsense. You are writing for a human audience, not robots, so your text and product description has to be targeted and make sense to people.

And I'll tell you what… if you don't, the robots that *do* read your page will notice this and act accordingly.

WHAT IS ON-PAGE SEO?

On-page SEO refers to things you can do to your website pages in order to optimize your SERP results.

SERP stands for search engine results page, which includes organic listings a search engine returns in response to a keyword query. In the SERP you will see a title and a brief description that will show where the keywords have matched the results.

Old-school thinking was to have those important keywords, usually in large numbers, as part of your content in order to influence search engines so your listing would appear closer to the top of the first results page.

That approach went the way of the dodo bird a while back.

But don't misunderstand. Keywords that are important to your description still carry some weight and, therefore, are important to a certain degree, but you cannot do what's referred to as "keyword stuffing" to improve SERP results.

Simply write descriptions naturally, and search engines will take care of the rest.

No. Your site will not suddenly jump ahead of everyone else's just because of this. There are many other factors at play here, but don't rely on old techniques that may end up hurting your site rather than helping it.

COMMON ON-PAGE SEO MISTAKES

These are just a few on-page SEO mistakes:

1. **Unoptimized title tags**—If your site has three hundred pages, for example, you ***must*** have three hundred unique title tags that clearly describe the page contents.

2. **Duplicate title tags**—Refer to item 1.

3. **Dead pages**—If you remove an item, make sure you don't leave dead links on your site.

4. **Hidden pages**—Every page on your site must be "crawlable" by search engine bots. Pages or sections that are confidential should be password-protected. You can also exclude them at the root of the domain through the robots.txt file.

5. **Duplicate content**—If you have the same content appearing on more than one page, do some editing. The same applies if you have copied and pasted content to your eBay store or blog for example.

6. **Too many links**—I've heard that over one hundred links are too much, regardless of page hierarchy.

7. **Lack of internal deep links**—Use some of your own link juice to bring new or deep pages to the attention of search engine bots.

8. **Targeting the wrong keywords**—Concentrate on the most valuable search terms for a particular product.

9. **A complex or deep category structure**—If your site's subcategories run over three deep, it's time to revise the architecture.

10. **Weak value proposition**—The purpose of your page and product or service must be clear. Aim to be better than your competition.

11. **Bad anchor text**—Use clear product descriptions when linking internally. Help visitors find stuff.

12. **Weak content**—Make sure your item descriptions provide good and relevant information to visitors.

13. **Typos and Grammatical Errors**—Google and Bing, for example, can spot them with ease, and that's a bad signal to them. There's no excuse for having typos and grammatical errors on your site.

14. **Slow-loading pages**—Text, code, and images (especially large graphics), must be optimized to load

fast without compromising quality.

15. **Poor site navigation**—A lack of common tools, such as a good menu bar, a sitemap, and breadcrumb trails, are a big hindrance to visitors, so make sure they are available.

16. **Poor or no text formatting**—The lack of "H" tags for headlines and subtitles, as well as a lack of bold and italic text, is unacceptable.

17. **Links to "bad" sites**—You'll have to do a little research on which sites are questionable, but as a general rule, avoid linking to anyone who asks you to "trade" links. And the same applies to someone offering to buy links from your site.

18. **Images with no ALT tags**—This is important and very easy to do. Add relevant ALT tags to all images.

19. **No CSS**—Cascading Style Sheets are important for many reasons, but as far as SEO goes, think of them as a set of instructions that allows search engines to locate the most relevant information easily.

20. **No Site Analytics**—Without knowing which pages are the most popular, which keywords generate traffic, and which sites bring customers to your site, you won't be able to focus on what works.

OFF-PAGE SEO

Off-page SEO, as the name implies, consists of strategies conducted on sites other than yours, and it's a technique that involves obtaining optimized links from external sites with hopes of improving SERP results.

WHAT IS OFF-PAGE SEO?

Off-page SEO usually involves link building from different sources: websites, social media, blogs, articles, and so on.

Think of links from external sites as the equivalent of "votes" for your site. At least that was the original idea. More links meant your site was popular.

That changed a few years ago, and now the quality of the links makes all the difference. In other words, an incoming link from a questionable blog is not the same as one from CNN, for example.

You have little control as far as off-page optimization is concerned. However, if you create a great website packed with good information, photos, videos, and links to valuable related information, off-page SEO will take care of itself.

Some may argue that pay per click (PPC), or any other form of online advertising, does qualify as off-page SEO, and I understand that the line separating PPC from off-page SEO is a fine and blurry one.

But for the purpose of this discussion, I will keep PPC and online advertising, in general, as a component of search engine marketing.

COMMON OFF-PAGE SEO MISTAKES

These are only a few off-page SEO mistakes, but the most common I see:

1. **Buying links**—You might as well paint a target on your back and forehead while you're at it, because buying links can be the kiss of death if you get caught.

2. **Unnatural links**—If your friend has a website or blog and links to you from every page to help you out, and the anchor text is full of keywords and long-tail search terms, you're asking for trouble. Many SEO "experts" use this approach on behalf of their clients. If your SEO is doing this, fire him!

3. **Blogs**—Having a blog for your site is a good idea, but if the only way for you to create one is through a free service, such as Blogger or WordPress, save your time and money. Any links coming from such a blog will work *against*, not *for* you. Your blog must be hosted on your site for it to be beneficial.

4. **Directory submissions**—Unless you are talking about important directories such as Yahoo! Directory

and Yelp, for example, avoid the thousands of obscure free-listing directories out there. Concentrate instead on the few that matter as well as any industry-relevant directories.

5. **Article marketing**—Another old technique that can hurt you. If you have a great article you would like to share with your audience, use your site's blog.

6. **Comment spam**—This is commentary posted on blogs and forums all over the web, regardless of relevancy. Another old technique used by some SEO "experts." If someone you hired is doing this on your behalf, fire them!

7. **Choosing quantity over quality**—You have to be picky about who you associate with. Don't waste time and resources trying to get as many sites as you can to link back to yours. Instead, focus on the very best, and work on getting those sites to mention yours, however they choose to. Links from authoritative websites are hundreds of times more valuable than links from questionable sites.

8. **Associating with link farms**—This technique is closely related to buying links, and it should be avoided like the plague. Any site containing pages with more than one hundred outgoing links is questionable.

9. **Don't trade links**—That technique is so last century. Don't trade links with anyone. Period.

10. **Press releases**—I truly believe this technique stopped working several years ago, so try it at your own risk.

11. **Social media**—Liking pages only to spam them with links to your site is almost infantile. Don't do it.

12. **Guest Blogging**—This questionable approach will take time and effort, and depending on the quality of the blog you are targeting, it may end up being a total waste of time. You have better things to do than act as a contributor to some obscure blog.

NEGATIVE SEO

This one is a difficult nut to crack since Google does not share much on the topic.

Negative SEO happens when a competitor does something like buying links to your site in a "bad neighborhood" or a "link farm," for example. The moment the Google algorithm notices, you could be in trouble.

Personally, I am curious as to why Google uses those questionable sites as a bad signal, especially considering that anyone can acquire links for a competitor with the intention of doing harm.

A few years ago, I read an article [1] by a "Googler" that explained that questionable links carried no weight and, therefore, did not help or hurt your site. However, a year or two after that article was published, Google enabled a "disavow" option on Google Webmaster Tools, which totally contradicts the previous claim.

I've also heard that Google has safety guards that prevent negative SEO from happening, but I am sure those safety guards are as effective as the ones claimed to keep PPC fraud under control.

Other forms of negative SEO include content scraping (which causes duplicate-content issues), fake negative reviews, negative forum comments about your company, services, products, or website, and more.

[1]   http://googlewebmastercentral.blogspot.com/2009/10/dealing-with-low-quality-backlinks.html

DISAVOW

Disavow really sounds like losing an inheritance, but in Google's case, it would allow you to (supposedly) disassociate your site from links pointing at it from "bad" sites. This would resolve, at least theoretically, the negative SEO scenario I mentioned previously.

Why Google chooses not to simplify this by not giving any weight to questionable sites, I do not know.

Google is obviously aware of these "bad" sites since they can penalize yours and then notify you of the action by issuing a warning e-mail through Webmaster Tools. However, they ask Webmasters to do the dirty and tedious work of, first, contacting the offending site to have it remove the links and, second, assuring it's been done or disavowing those sites that do not comply.

What's wrong with that picture?

If your site has links from questionable sites pointing at it, you may want to take immediate action to disavow them. However, be warned that the process is slow and difficult, and you may need a real professional to get the job done correctly in the eyes of Google.

IS SEO DEAD?

I believe the answer is yes—at least as far as the traditional spamming approaches are concerned. What's left of it is on life support. And from the looks of it, Google is willing to pull the plug at any time.

SEO pundits will argue that statement, and who can blame them? Their livelihood depends on it. And as long as website owners everywhere are in a panic, they'll stay busy.

Actually, most SEOs have started combining SEO with web marketing (something at which they also excel, of course).

And so...

SEM IS BORN

Search engine marketing (SEM) is self-explanatory and the latest "must have" for anyone who owns or operates a website, especially a commercial site.

According to Wikipedia,

> *Search engine marketing (SEM) is a form of Internet marketing that involves the promotion of websites by increasing their visibility in search engine results pages (SERPs) through optimization and advertising. SEM may use search engine optimization (SEO) that adjusts or rewrites website content to achieve a higher ranking in search engine results pages or use pay per click listings.*
>
> —"Search engine marketing," *Wikipedia,* http://en.wikipedia.org/wiki/Search_engine_marketing

And search engine marketing does not stop there.

You can also buy services for:

- Search branding
- Local search marketing
- Mobile search marketing

And who knows what else.

WHAT IS SEM?

SEM is nothing new, and it's been around for more than a decade.

In its most basic form, search engine marketing (SEM) is buying ads on search engines. However, SEM also has other components that go beyond PPC and display advertising.

I believe it is safe to say that SEM is, for the most part, nothing more than buying web traffic or potential customers. However, the acronym sounds a lot better. But unless you purchase targeted traffic, you will end up wasting money.

Back in the late 1990s, there was a company called GoTo.com which pioneered the pay-per-click (PPC) advertising concept.

Since I was selling motorcycle repair manuals online at the time, I decided to go ahead and purchase some ads. But being a total newbie at online marketing, I bought ads that would show up for the word "motorcycle."

I set up my one hundred dollar budget which, at the time, was a sizeable investment for me, and started my first PPC campaign.

Do I have to tell you my budget was depleted in under an hour or did you already guess?

I learned about "targeted searches" the hard way, but since it was back when we were all learning new things about the online world, I guess I can be forgiven for that mistake.

SEM can also include other venues.

- Web directories
- Shopping search
- Social media
- Press releases
- Article marketing
- Blogging
- Guest blogging
- Public relations

And more.

Does your site need all these approaches?

Probably not, but some "experts" may disagree and sell you...
I mean, *tell you* otherwise.

COMMON SEM MISTAKES

There are many things that can go wrong with SEM
techniques, especially those involving PPC. And many of
them may actually hurt your search engine ranking.

Remember that just because something worked fine before,
it does not mean that it will work well today. Common SEM
mistakes include the following:

- Bidding on the wrong keywords

- Failing to test which keywords have the best return on investment (ROI)

- Using highly competitive keywords

- Misusing keyword match types

- Failing to target the correct geographical areas. If the majority of your customers are in the United States and Canada, for example, you have to target those markets specifically.

- Poorly-designed landing pages

- Sending traffic to 404 pages

- Sending traffic to irrelevant pages

- Using bad ad copy

- Failing to use negative keywords

- Not being involved in the PPC process (No one knows your business better than you.)

- Using traffic numbers as the key metric

- Setting the campaigns, and then failing to monitor their performance. Don't just "set it and forget it."

- Buying links in questionable directories

- Buying followers for social media sites

- Not using mobile marketing correctly

- Spinning articles

- Not having and following a well-defined marketing plan

- Uploading useless videos to YouTube

- Not using the right analysis tools

- Ignoring Bing PPC

- Failing to use Google Local and Google Maps (if your business also serves a local clientele)

WHO CAN YOU TRUST?

I'm not saying I don't trust you, and I'm not saying I do. But I don't.
—Topper Harley, *Hot Shots! Part Deux* (1993)

Someone I greatly respect once told me he conducts business only with people or companies when *he* initiates contact. I consider that valuable advice and most applicable in this case.

When I owned my web store, not a day would go by without either an e-mail or a phone call from someone trying to sell me SEO services.

Those are the ones to avoid.

If you really want or need the services of a reputable SEO company, finding one is not difficult. There are many lists available online with the names of companies or individuals who know their stuff well, but you will have to do some research. You will also have to ensure that the source of that information is trustworthy.

Research takes time, but you have to conduct due diligence when you are considering making a financial investment of any kind, especially when it is SEO related.

And keep in mind that anyone can give you a great résumé.

In all my years as a business owner, I read many résumés, but never a bad one.

HIRING AN SEO FIRM

Every company is different, so your budget will determine the amount of work they can or will do for you.

A few may have long-term contract requirements, and since every situation is different, that may be what your site needs, so I won't tell you to walk away when someone presents that scenario to you.

Hiring an SEO firm is like choosing a doctor when dealing with a serious condition. I would get at least two, if not three, different opinions.

Some SEO firms are owned by people who are really good at their job, but I can almost guarantee that you will end up dealing with an employee. Not a bad thing, necessarily, but if you feel like you're purchasing a used car, go to the next one.

I spent thousands of dollars on a big-name firm. The owner sold me on his credentials, and they were impressive. He knew all the right people and is well respected within the search industry.

I believe I spoke with him the first two times when I was on the fence about who to hire. After that, I dealt with one of his employees who, although a very nice, knowledgeable, and thorough person, did little to help me improve my situation. I felt tricked since after the $7,000 check was cashed, Mr. Big Name was obviously too busy to talk with me.

You should always ask for referrals, but know that you will be given the ones that they feel are worth talking to. I doubt that anyone would allow you to talk with an unsatisfied customer.

Conducting online searches for complaints about SEO firms, especially the ones you are considering, may prove to be time well spent.

Since it is likely you will have to sign some form of a contract or agreement, you may want to have your attorney read it. Remember that the SEO firm's attorney wrote the contract they want you to sign.

The contract should list exactly what they will do for you and the time frame required. But understand that time will not be on your side, and just because you or someone you hired made changes to your site—or whatever else they changed—that doesn't mean search engines will update SERPs based on your schedule.

Changes can take anywhere from a few days to months to reflect on SERPs. In spite of how fast data travels on the Internet today, search engines are usually slow at making directory or index updates.

2014-AND-BEYOND SEO FIRMS

SEO used to be a one-size-fits-all industry. That approach no longer works.

Using my previous example on choosing a doctor, when it comes to the health of your online efforts, you need a specialist.

What I mean by that is if, for example, your site caters to motorcycle lovers, you want an SEO firm that understands that market completely so it knows how to communicate with your core audience.

If you are considering an SEO agency and all its agents talk about are keywords, keyword density, incoming links from authoritative sites, and stuff that was popular during the first decade of the twenty-first century, that agency is not for you.

You need either an individual or company that lives and breathes the motorcycling lifestyle, or whatever your industry may be. The person or company you hire needs to be deeply connected and in tune with your company and philosophy so you both operate in the same frequency. Otherwise it will be a formula for disaster.

In order to become an authority at your trade, you need a great support system. You cannot afford to have someone in your team that does not know your industry as an enthusiast.

If someone other than you will be the "voice" of your company, that representative needs to speak the "language." Otherwise your authority and credibility will dissolve almost instantly.

The new SEO world is changing rapidly by becoming industry-centric, something that was long overdue.

And the same approach applies when outsourcing PPC advertising and Internet video production for example.

Get used to the idea that you will need a specialist in your industry. If you don't consider that important, the next time you have an ingrown toenail go see a dentist, and let me know how that works out for you.

SEO in 2014 and beyond is a different environment. Whereas a few years ago you would ask your SEO to "fix" your site by helping it rank for a few keywords or perform on- or off-page "tricks," those simplistic approaches are no longer valid.

You are the "key ingredient" in the new search world, so you have to be involved.

THE SILVER BULLET

Just like the werewolves it was designed to kill, the "silver bullet" is fictional, and if your site has been adversely impacted by Google, then you will be faced with some tough decisions.

- Do you hire a good and qualified SEO firm?
- Do you try to fix it yourself?
- Do you launch a new site?

None are guaranteed to quickly or cheaply solve the problems you may be experiencing. And you will have to make the decision as to which one is the better alternative.

If the penalties against your site are unsurmountable, you may need to take a deep breath and start from scratch. But you need someone good to help you find the right answer and understand what it will take. So option number one, hiring a good, qualified SEO firm, is probably where you need to start.

However, before you start searching for a good SEO firm, you have to do a little homework.

1. What is your daily traffic?

2. How much time are visitors spending on your site?

3. What percentage of visitors actually makes a purchase?

4. Which products do they buy?

5. Do they get to the landing page from an external link or through an internal site search?

6. What is the preferred shipping method?

7. How many of these best sellers do you ship out per week? Per month?

8. Where are these buyers located?

9. Which are the referring sites?

10. Are the purchasers referred from organic listings, or are they coming to your site from PPC campaigns?

These are a few of the questions you—as a business owner—should have answers for.

Those answers may, in fact, be a "silver bullet" of sorts. Maybe not the large caliber you need or would like to have in order to slay the big bad *algos*—disguised as cute birds and animals—that may be trashing your site.

Armed with this intelligence, you can start formulating a plan to replicate and also improve on your results.

I am going to assume that you have at least one spreadsheet that lists all your expenses and contains fields for sales data, which tell you exactly what you need to be selling in order to be profitable. This spreadsheet should be one of the tools you refer to daily, and it also should allow you to play with the numbers so you have targets to shoot for.

You see, at the end of the day, if you make only a few bucks after all the bills and salaries have been paid, you made money! You are profitable! But you need to be in absolute control of the numbers so you can tell, without a shadow of a doubt, if you are making or losing money.

Don't allow your brain to play tricks on you. It's very easy to get into a panic when you are wondering if you will have enough money to pay the electric bill this month.

Anxiety is caused by the belief that things or situations are beyond our control.

You should also have an up-to-date spreadsheet for your personal income and expenses. And if you are not proficient with Excel, spend a few bucks and get some training online from Lynda.com or buy a *For Dummies* book.

Once you have your spreadsheet ready, you can have some fun figuring out how much more money you will make if you sell an additional number of items each month. And, of course, you will know what the bottom line is.

Just make sure that your data is accurate, and understand that your spreadsheet will be a work in progress as you continue to fine-tune it.

READY, AIM, FIRE

Now that you have a better understanding of your finances, you can start making some decisions.

As you know, expenses will be paid from profits you make.

Start by formulating a strategy to sell more of those products that are selling well. I would create another spreadsheet just to have a clear picture of all the data you collect about your store traffic and sales performance.

This will allow you to concentrate on those items that are best sellers for you so you can optimize them even more. Plus, knowing how customers find these best sellers will be instrumental.

If you determine that customers who purchase certain items are coming from organic listings, you then have a crucial piece of information. And that "success formula" is something you have to decode. Sort of a reverse-engineering process.

There are some elements both on-site and off-site that are bringing in customers, and you have to do your best to figure out what those elements are.

The same formula applies to buyers of items who are referred through PPC. Study those ads carefully, and try to determine what the "secret" may be.

Once you figure out the answers to these questions, you can start by testing the same approach on other items, and see if your theories hold water. If they don't, modify them a bit and try again.

But don't make site-wide changes without testing things first. As a matter of fact, I would advise against making universal changes to your site since what works for one product may not apply to another.

Test, test again, then test some more.

Develop a methodology that works and put it to good use. Just make sure that you have a system in place, and follow each step in the right order.

Go back to your spreadsheet and try to improve results with attainable goals. Doing so will help you develop parameters for products so you can focus on those that generate a good return on investment.

SOCIAL MEDIA

I believe that unless you are willing to spend the time and effort to maintain a current and up-to-date social presence, you are better off waiting until you are ready.

There are plenty of useless Facebook, Twitter, LinkedIn, Pinterest, Google+, Tumblr, and Instagram pages on the net, and you don't want to add to that effort.

The only conclusion one can make is that by publishing garbage as a justification for having a social networking channel, all you accomplish is helping the sites that provide the services by giving them content.

I am sure a few "experts" will argue that a social presence is a must, and, therefore, you have to launch such pages, quality be damned.

Some may even promise you a constant stream of "likes" or followers as part of their services. Do not fall for that one. For social networks to be valuable, they have to grow organically. Besides, having tens of thousands of followers that fail to interact with your site is pathetic, and it may raise a red flag to search engine bots that keep getting smarter by the hour, or so it seems.

Will not having a social media channel hurt you?

I really don't believe so. And like I said before, having a social media channel "just because" can be far worse.

When you are ready to launch one, I suggest you start with Google+.

I am not against Facebook, but I consider Google+ a better choice both audience- and platform-wise, and Google made the announcement in early 2012, that its search results would include Google+ through "Social Search Integration."

BLOGS

A blog is another channel that—just like social media—is considered by many SEO "experts" an indispensable tool to help your site climb the organic SERPs ladder.

If you create a blog just to help your organic rankings, you are so far off course, it's not even funny.

Instead of wasting time creating additional channels, spend the time and energy working on your website, and improve it by writing unique and significant content and making it user-friendly.

Like I mentioned before, if you need a blog for your site, it's not going to hurt, and it may prove helpful as far as search engines are concerned, but do not start one for that reason. Your blog must be an extension of your site, and you must have a subdomain for it, such as http://blog.mydomain.com.

Do not use Blogger or other third-party services to create one, even if you have a dedicated URL for it. Your blog should be a part of your site. Otherwise, you may end up creating something that looks like a "link wheel," with negative consequences.

PAY PER CLICK

Pay per click (PPC) is a form of advertising. It can also be referred to as cost per click (CPC).

With pay-per-click, you are buying space on a search engine, and your ads will be shown on the first page (sometimes on page one and two) when the keywords you specified trigger the ad to appear.

Based on how much you are able to spend for each click, your ad may appear higher than other competing ads since most PPC systems operate on a bid basis.

Conversely, if you are willing to pay up to thirty-five cents for a search term, for example, and your competitor bids thirty-six cents, then your ad may show up below his or hers. I say "may" because there are other factors at play with PPC advertising.

PPC advertising can get you noticed very quickly, and unlike organic results, you are pretty much guaranteed a spot on the first page.

However, there are factors that can make PPC advertising unappealing to many merchants. Things such as click fraud can be a serious problem, although the big search engines claim to have safety measures in place to prevent that from happening.

Another concern is that because it is based on a bidding system, some people can get carried away as to how much they are willing to pay for each click. So some keywords and search terms may be out of your reach due to unreasonable bids.

PPC advertising has gotten very complex, to the point that large companies have dedicated staff that manages their campaigns. There are many companies and freelancers that offer PPC management, but you have to be very careful when farming out these tasks.

I used the services of one of these so-called "pros" a few years ago. One day, while checking the campaigns he had created, I discovered he was bidding on keywords for products we did not carry. Mistakes like that can cost you hundreds or thousands of dollars.

There are companies that use a performance-based model. In other words, they only profit based on how your campaigns perform. A few others use a crowdsourcing model where you get the combined thinking power of a group of people. And yet others may use a combination of the two.

But keep in mind that "performance" will mean different things for you than it will for them when it comes to evaluating the success level of your campaigns.

For the company offering the service, click-through traffic will probably be the measure of their success. To you, sales and profitability of the campaigns will be the metric that will matter.

For most small businesses, PPC is a task that works best when done in-house, ideally by the business owner.

RATINGS AND FEEDBACK

Amazon figured out this important piece of the e-commerce puzzle years before other merchants did and has used it masterfully for achieving prominent positioning on SERPs and helping customers make a purchase.

This chapter is the most important part of SEO and something you won't have to relinquish to the "experts."

You will gain the most benefit by having customers give you feedback on the products they purchase, and you will also derive benefits if they not only rate the products but also rate you as the merchant.

Product feedback and ratings should be integrated into the respective items, and I would position them right after the product description.

This commentary, provided by people who purchased the product, is not only extremely valuable from an SEO perspective but is even more important as a sales tool, since most of us are influenced by the opinions of others.

But what if you are just getting bad reviews for a particular item? Simple—do not carry merchandise people dislike.

No one likes to buy useless stuff. It's not only a waste of money but also a waste of time.

Also consider the benefits of having your customers help you trim the fat out of your inventory. That is valuable information, and you should tailor your offerings based on products your customers like and use. The rest should be liquidated and never stocked again.

Having said that, negative feedback is appropriate, even helpful, as it provides credibility for your website.

Product feedback is the equivalent of "cyber gold" as far as your site is concerned, and you should consider investing time and resources to give it the prominence it deserves. So find ways to get as many product reviews as possible, positive, negative, and neutral, as they are all valuable for you and your customers.

Product feedback should be very prominent. I understand that because of design considerations, sometimes a tab may be more appropriate for feedback. Do not use that approach. Feedback should be front and center.

I also understand that you must set some parameters in case you get tens or hundreds of comments, but only resort to tabs or other alternatives when that becomes an issue. And I would always keep at least five feedback comments on the page.

Feedback must be one hundred percent related to the item. Don't just paste generic text thinking that it will help you. It may actually have the exact opposite effect.

Don't mess this one up.

GENERATING FEEDBACK

Every product category is different, and some items may lend themselves more easily to generating customer feedback or comments than others.

The easiest way to get people to participate is to provide the tools necessary for feedback. A simple form on product pages may work wonders for this, and it is something that you should discuss with your website developer in order to implement.

An e-mail may also be effective and when combined with social media channels, probably a way to motivate customers to share their thoughts. A discount coupon for future purchases may also help generate a higher rate of responses.

Even a contest asking for brief product reviews where the winner gets a cash prize, for example, may provide enough unique and valuable content for your site.

When customers call, ask them for a few comments about what they bought from you, write those comments down, and then add them to your site.

Just remember that each review or feedback must be laser-accurate for each product, and placed alongside the corresponding item.

Product feedback must be text so it can be read by both humans and bots. Avoid images or JavaScript code. Just plain HTML should do the trick.

NUQ HOL DAJATLH'A'?

If you don't understand the heading above, it could be written in Klingon for all you know, and, indeed, it is written in the language of the Klingon Empire.

I admit that I used the Bing translator since I don't speak Klingon, but it's amazing the stuff you can find online. An English-to-Klingon translator!

Language is a crucial element when it comes to correctly describing products. Things such as colloquialisms may be important to something you may be selling, but a lot can be lost in translation. It is very easy to get lured into hiring someone through a service like Elance.com who may not be a native English speaker, and that could be a critical error.

Content production is too important, and not an area where you want to cut corners.

Even when it comes to American versus British English, the differences can be huge. I think George Bernard Shaw said it best when he quipped, *"England and America are two countries separated by a common language."*

I am not picking on anyone with this statement; this rule applies to any and all languages. Each country has its own nuances, and they can make a huge difference when it comes to website content.

Write for your audience, and do not take shortcuts that can only be justified as futile attempts at saving a few bucks.

PAGE AUTHORITY

*I have as much authority as the Pope; I just
don't have as many people who believe it.*
—George Carlin

Page authority is a term used by the SEO industry, and its main purpose is to help determine the chances that a specific page on your site will appear on search engine result pages.

Like with most things SEO, page authority is confusing since it is usually thrown around along with PageRank, a quality metric invented by Larry Page and Sergey Brin, founders of Google.

I am unable to tell you whether either of these metrics matter as far as SERPs are concerned, but they seem to be helpful to those trying to sell you SEO services. As far as Google is concerned, they won't tell anyone what these metrics accomplish, so I would not give them much thought.

If you build helpful pages, your customers will consider your site the "authority" on the subject, and isn't that what really matters?

SEARCH WITHIN SEARCH

A consultant from a very prominent SEO firm told me a couple of years ago that Google does not look favorably upon "search within search." In other words, when Google sends someone to a specific page within your site and that person has to search again, using your site's search engine to locate a certain item, Google does not care for that.

I consider this a valuable and credible piece of information that makes perfect sense. Google (and other search engines) wants to provide the most accurate results with as few clicks as possible—one click being the ultimate goal.

In order for that to happen, your pages must be optimized correctly, so when someone lands on a page, it provides the answer to whatever the searcher was looking for.

Having said that, you need to make site search available to your visitors regardless of what Google thinks. Ultimately, your site should be designed for human beings, not search engine bots, and usability is crucial if you want to provide a good user experience. Besides, Google is not the only game in town.

Even though Bing's search percentage compared to Google's is much smaller, the truth of the matter is that as small of a percentage as it may be, it still translates into millions of daily visitors, and you want to cater to them also.

SCHEMA AND CANONICAL TAGS

Schema and canonical tags are something you will need to discuss with your service provider and website developer. Some platforms may do this type of tagging automatically while others may not.

Schema tags, for example, are HTML tags that you can use to markup your pages to help large search engines, such as Google, Bing, and Yahoo!, with indexing and search results.

The schema initiative was launched by Google, Bing, and Yahoo! in 2011 in order to "create and support a common set of schemas for structured data markup on web pages."

Canonical tags, which are also supported by the largest search engines, are intended to help eliminate duplicate-content issues.

Since both schema and canonical are HTML tags, you can check your site's source code to see if they are in place. If they are not, talk to your provider.

For more details visit:

- http://www.schema.org
- http://bit.ly/1dkJjCi

ALGOS

A search algo, or algorithm, is basically a computer program or a formula that determines which listings will appear as the most relevant on search engine result pages (SERPs).

Search engine algos are well-kept secrets and their formulas only known to a select few, so when it comes to search engine algos, everyone guesses, and while some of these estimates may be more educated and accurate than others, they still are a guess.

Some of the most recent and popular (or evil, depending on how they treated your site) Google algorithms and their primary focus, follow:

PANDA

- Website quality and user experience
- Website trustworthiness
- Quality of content

PENGUIN

- Adherence to Google Webmaster Guidelines
- No gray- or black-hat SEO techniques
- Artificial manipulation of inbound links
- No article spam
- No links schemes

EMD (Exact Match Domain)

- Keyword domain names
- Keyword-heavy content
- Overall quality of "exact match" website

HUMMINGBIRD

- Social media signals
- Mobile versions of websites
- Semantic search

The focus of algorithms, as itemized above, is based solely on my research on the subject and is not an official guide. You are encouraged to investigate and read more on the subject to learn the specifics of each program and draw your own conclusions.

THE GOOGLE SANDBOX

Just like Bigfoot, Google's sandbox existence has been confirmed by many an SEO expert and hotly contested by others.

Some define it as a penalty box or a "time-out" for naughty Webmasters. I've also heard that the sandbox is where new sites sit until Google decides whether they'll be indexed and thus included on the SERPs.

As far as I know, Google has neither confirmed nor denied its existence, so your guess is as good as mine.

Why bother mentioning it then?

Well, if you haven't heard about it already, you may hear the term at some point from an SEO "expert," which should give you pause and good reason to question the source of the information you may be receiving.

WHAT SHOULD YOU FOCUS ON?

Much like with Panda and Penguin, after Hummingbird was released, some websites lost half or more of their traffic. That's huge, and to many website owners, catastrophic.

No one has the perfect recovery formula, but here are a few of my recommendations, based on my research and experience, for your consideration:

- Unique accurate content and information is a key element. You must provide it not only for search engines but especially for your readership.

- Do some house cleaning and get rid of dead pages and simplify your site's navigation.

- As a content creator, you need to have author credentials established with Google and link any articles or other content you create with your Google+ profile. https://plus.google.com/authorship

- Do keyword research and testing, but stop thinking that you should rank number one for every keyword. Keywords are not important search engine signals as they used to be ten or so years ago.

- Learn how to use Google Analytics. It is a powerful program and you, as a Webmaster, should devote the time necessary to use it properly.

- Learn how to use and interpret your website logs to determine which pages are popular and which keywords and pages are making you money. Also very important is to determine how visitors are finding your site. Maybe you shouldn't be worrying only about pleasing Google. Bing and other sites may be contributing far more traffic, so make sure you know who is bringing people to your site.

- A mobile version of your website nowadays is not only important but imperative. Don't wait any longer to develop a mobile site.

- Talk to your developer about having a "responsive" website, which can be viewed properly, regardless of platform.

- You have to provide a great website with usable and unique content, great photos and images, and links to relevant sites.

- After taking good care of your website, consider a social media channel. Google+ is a good idea since you should already have your author profile established. Facebook, of course, is another excellent social media channel as is Pinterest.

- If appropriate, start your own YouTube channel, but remember to use it for the benefit of your customers and readership.

YOUR UNIQUE SELLING PROPOSITION

Regardless of what you may be selling, I can almost guarantee that you will have lots of competition from big stores, such as Amazon and Walmart, to small businesses. And let's not forget the "weekend warriors" selling the same stuff on eBay or Craigslist.

So it is crucial for you to determine what your unique selling proposition (USP) is. This is a key factor and something you must use to make your business stand head and shoulders above the competition.

These are just a few USP ideas:

- Free shipping
- Same-day shipping
- Open seven days a week
- Free gift with order
- Portion of profits support a cause

I left "lowest price" off the list, since that's something almost everyone claims and it's a bad formula for reaching profitability. So use your creativity. Ask your friends what motivates them to purchase stuff online. What makes them decide to shop at certain stores.

Get as much information as you can in order to formulate a plan and your USP. Once you have it, start promoting it, and become known for it.

GO LOCAL

If the service you provide or the merchandise you sell is available to a local clientele, you should optimize your website so it appears in Google, Bing, and Yahoo! local searches.

Local or geographical optimization goes beyond keywords, and you should include a "land" address (street, city, and zip code). A post office box does not qualify. Additionally, you can also include latitude and longitude coordinates, which can be helpful for a mobile search.

Make it easy for local customers or clients to find you, so optimize your website for "local search."

This may not be possible if you work from home, of course, but if your business is a serious enterprise, then maybe the time has come to move it out of the third bedroom or garage and rent a small office or storefront in town.

I have nothing against home-based businesses. I launched my company from home, but once it expanded beyond the garage and guest bedroom, I purchased a small office in town and never looked back.

Over the years, we sold many books over-the-counter as local customers found our address and stopped by our office to pick up their purchases. Most of them found us thanks to our search engine "local" pages.

RUN THE VIRTUAL VACUUM

Fresh content is a key element if you want your site to remain significant and continue ranking well. This is not easy to accomplish, and constantly refreshing pages can be a gargantuan task, especially if your site has a lot of pages.

But it is important, and you should have a plan on how to keep the most important (and profitable) pages fresh and up-to-date.

That's where customer feedback is crucial; customers give you fresh, new content, which allows you to update those pages with little effort. That's also why I think feedback should be on the same page as the product description and, if possible, above the fold.

To give you a basic example, think of a blog. New posts appear first, even though the timeline is being displayed backward.

I strongly recommend that you give fresh content, such as feedback, a prime spot, even if it's only a snippet.

Make it a habit to get rid of stale content, add new photos, rearrange the text, and add customers' feedback. Maybe include new videos and podcasts. This will ensure your pages are always fresh and remain interesting.

JACK OF ALL TRADES

If you are going to try to play the game by Google's rules, you will have to be prepared to not only set up a web store but also make sure it's designed properly, with unique and engaging content.

You will also be in charge of marketing and social media efforts and maintaining up-to-date Facebook and (especially) Google+ pages. Additional tasks may include giving interviews to local papers and relevant blogs. You will also produce and star in your own YouTube videos, which will help you tell the story of your company.

Not sure how you plan to squeeze in there to fulfill orders and run a business while still having a life, but algorithms don't care about that. It's all about quality content with them.

Is it all worth it? You be the judge.

I am sure Bing and others are paying close attention to what's happening here, and while I do not disagree that enough is enough with all the SEO "experts," there has to be a better and fairer system for search engines to provide meaningful results.

Being a public company, Google operates by a different set of rules, and as long as shareholders are happy, everything is well with the universe. But if history repeats itself—as it usually does—a couple of kids in a garage somewhere may be in the process of inventing a better search engine.

GAMING THE SYSTEM

Nearly all men can stand adversity, but if you want to test a man's character, give him power.
—Abraham Lincoln

There is no question that Google has gotten too big and too powerful. I believe that competition fosters growth, but that is nearly impossible today because of the large share of web search commandeered by Google.

And while I cannot disagree that we have to rid the web of all the SEO charlatans who are doing more harm than good, I don't believe that only one company should be entrusted with the process.

The idea of having intelligent algorithms in the future that feed us the "best" results based on the opinion of a committee is not only fascinating but scary. What happens then with political websites and dissident opinions? Will those views also be censored based on the opinions of the few who write these algorithms?

That topic is material for another book, of course, but it is something to ponder.

Getting back on track, anything anyone does in order to make his or her site better, more popular, or successful, will be considered—at one point or another—an attempt to game the system.

We are damned whether we do or don't.

Regardless of how many "right" things you do, there will be one or two or more that will be "wrong" at some point or another, so go back to basics, and use your energy to build the best website or web store you can. Do it for yourself and your customers.

And don't get swindled by SEO "experts" who promise you solutions that are nothing more than fantasies. They will tell you what you want to hear and bill you for their services, of course, but that won't solve any of your problems.

If you operate an e-commerce website, you're better off investing time and money on pay-per-click advertising. There are many good books available on the subject and a ton of free information online, so read up on the subject and optimize your PPC campaigns.

And if you have not explored selling through other channels, such as Amazon's Marketplace and eBay, you owe it to yourself to research those venues, especially considering the huge amount of traffic they generate.

I am not necessarily suggesting you give up your regular website in favor of an Amazon or eBay web store, but they have the potential to be viable supplements to your e-commerce efforts and should not be ignored.

Amazon is a very attractive platform since it also allows you to build a web store and use its warehouses for product fulfillment. Because of economies of scale, Amazon can actually save you money on shipping charges. Plus, you can also save on or eliminate overhead costs, shipping materials, and more.

In addition, you can also benefit from Amazon Prime, which is a service many of Amazon's customers use and love. You receive merchandise in two days and with free shipping. What's not to love about that?

One of the key advantages offered by Amazon and eBay is that their traffic is comprised mainly of shoppers. If you want buyers for whatever it is you are selling, you need to make your wares available to the right audience.

CHOOSE YOUR HAT CAREFULLY

The other day, as I was checking Amazon for the listing of *Add to Cart Tuneup*, my first book, I saw a bunch of suggestions at the bottom of the page.

Some, if not most, of the books were totally worthless and full of SEO information that was okay in and around 2002 but not so much today. As a matter of fact, some of the suggestions would be considered "black hat" SEO by any of the large search engines.

My point is to be careful about where you get your SEO information from. I believe I have made my point that there is very little you or anyone else can do for your site as far as tricking the search engines, especially Google, when it comes to gray- or black-hat techniques.

If you get caught—and the chances of that taking place are higher than ever—your site will be penalized to the extent that you may have to start over with a clean slate. That's too high of a price to pay, in my opinion.

So you've been warned. And if you come across articles, books, or e-books with titles that babble about generating tons of traffic for your site, how to get to the number one spot on Google, SEO secrets, and other fiction like that, ignore them.

Good and accurate information is available out there. You just have to be willing to do a little research and be selective. And like the old saying goes, "If it sounds too good to be true, it probably is."

PARTING THOUGHTS

I read a while ago that many of the engineers who work in Google's search department are *Star Trek* fans, which is no surprise. Like a lot of *Star Trek* fans, I loved the original series as well as *Star Trek: The Next Generation* and *Star Trek: Voyager*.

I wish humankind was at that level.

Unfortunately, at this point, a large portion of the world population seems to be more aligned with the Ferengi instead, a fictional extraterrestrial race obsessed with profit and trade.

I don't think Gene Roddenberry would be proud or happy.

To those of you who believe that one day we'll live up to a higher level of consciousness, service to others, and honor— in the words of Spock, "Live long and prosper."

Thank you for reading.

Luis Hernandez, Jr.

ABOUT THE AUTHOR

Luis launched his first website in 1995, followed by an online bookstore specializing in motorcycle literature in 1997.

He lives in Orange City, Florida.

This is his second book.

FEEDBACK

If you have comments, thoughts, or ideas you'd like to discuss or share on the subject, please visit
www.LuisHernandezJr.com

On LinkedIn, visit
www.linkedin.com/in/lhernandezjr/

On Google+, visit:
https://plus.google.com/+LuisHernandezJr/posts